THE
HEALING
GAME

A VIETNAM SOLDIER'S STORY

CHARLES LOUIS SINGLETON

AuthorHouse™
1663 Liberty Drive
Bloomington, IN 47403
www.authorhouse.com
Phone: 833-262-8899

Because of the dynamic nature of the Internet, any web addresses or links contained in this book may have changed since publication and may no longer be valid. The views expressed in this work are solely those of the author and do not necessarily reflect the views of the publisher, and the publisher hereby disclaims any responsibility for them.

Any people depicted in stock imagery provided by Getty Images are models, and such images are being used for illustrative purposes only.
Certain stock imagery © Getty Images.

This book is printed on acid-free paper.

ISBN: 978-1-6655-6613-1 (sc)
ISBN: 978-1-6655-6615-5 (hc)
ISBN: 978-1-6655-6614-8 (e)

Library of Congress Control Number: 2022913710

Print information available on the last page.

Published by AuthorHouse 07/26/2022

authorHOUSE®

THE HEALING GAME

A VIETNAM SOLDIER'S STORY

CHARLES LOUIS SINGLETON
Summerville, South Carolina, 1970–1971, SNB, RVN
US Army, Noncommissioned Officer
NCO Shake and Bake Sergeant, Fort Benning, Georgia, 1970

Sgt. Charles L. Singleton, US Army, Tour 365, May 25, 1970–April 25, 1971, Republic of Vietnam Service Christmas card, Vietnam, First Team Productions. Other photos are in the public domain.

US Army Vietnam soldiers in line to get in a plane for a combat mission

RICHARD M. NIXON, 1969

It is beyond question that without the American commitment in Vietnam, Asia would be a far different place today . . . Asian leaders know why we are in Vietnam . . . and urge us to see it through to a satisfactory conclusion.

LYNDON B. JOHNSON, 1965

The central issue of the conflict . . . is the aggression by North Vietnam. . . . If that aggression is stopped, the people and government of South Vietnam will be free to settle their own future and get on with the great tasks of national development.

JOHN F. KENNEDY, 1961

. . . The United States is determined to help Vietnam preserve its independence, protect its people against Communist assassins, and build a better life through economic growth.

DWIGHT D. EISENHOWER, 1959

The loss of South Vietnam would set in motion a crumbling process that could, as it progressed, have consequences for us and for freedom.

TOUR 365

For Soldiers Going Home

Contents for Summer 1970 Issue

Tour 365 is an authorized publication of the United States Army, Vietnam. It is published under the supervision of the Information Officer, USARV, APO San Francisco 96375, semi-annually for distribution to the soldiers returning to the United States upon completion of their tour in the Republic of Vietnam. Opinions expressed herein are not necessarily those of the Department of Defense or Department of the Army. The following agencies are thanked for their valuable contributions to the production of Tour 365: Military History Branch, USARV; Command Historian, USARV; U.S. Army Pictorial Center; Pacific Stars & Stripes for permission to use a condensation of a review of 1968 action which appeared in Pacific Stars & Stripes Magazine, and to those past and present members of the USARV Information Office staff for their editorial contributions.

General Creighton W. Abrams, Commanding General
Lieutenant General Frank T. Mildren, Deputy Commanding General
Lieutenant Colonel Ross L. Johnson, Information Officer
Major Victor F. Keefe, Command Information Officer
First Lieutenant Joseph E. Moreland Jr., Editor
Sergeant Alex Van Ryan, Associate Editor

Tour 365, Republic of Vietnam Service, US Army, summer 1970, APO San Francisco.

A Vietnam Soldier's Story, US Army, First Cavalry Division, Airmobile, Sgt. Charles L. Singleton, NCO Shake and Bake Sergeant, South Vietnam, 1970–1971, Tahesha Brown, literary DVD PowerPoint technical consultant.

Dr. Charles L. Singleton, author of *Read Between the Lines, Windows of Recourse: Provocative Essays for Saving Our Children and Their Precious Lives* (1997, 2019), is a contributing coauthor of Robert O. "Bob" Babcock's Vietnam Books, *I'm Ready to Talk* and *I'm Ready to Talk Two* (2020, 2022).

Singleton has written 120 family journal entries, 95 nationally and locally published articles, 5 scholastic fitness and adult tennis players annotated record booklets, 2 collegiate and clinical research annotated booklets, 105 years of *The Family Journal, USA & Overseas Military Historical Service,* more than 100 in memoriam tributes, and highlighted more than 30 YouTube–produced Celebration of Life gospel songs.

Charles Singleton's historical reflections and scholarly leadership (1968) at Elizabeth City State College (ECSC), Elizabeth City, North Carolina: "Student Nonviolent Response," and Student Council President, Charles Singleton (1967–1968), Summerville, South Carolina, page 216: "A peaceful nonviolent ECSC march and celebration of life, and we stayed in school after the assassination of Martin Luther King Jr., April 4, 1968."

ECSU professor of history Dr. Glen Bowman's historical review, "From Confrontation: Student Activism at Elizabeth City State Teachers/State College, 1948–1968," the *North Carolina Historical Review* 98, no. 2 (April 2021). Singleton's journalism is highlighted in the book *African Americans on Tour, History, People and Places of Summerville, South Carolina*, by Linda Saylor-Marchant and Violet Saylor, 2022.

Edited by
Designed by
First edition

Special thanks to more than a hundred family members, friends, classmates, and associates. Read more: *The Republic of Vietnam under Attack. Vietnam Soldier's Journey.*

Charles L. Singleton (1968–1969), Charles and Samuel Houston Charles, and Savath Som—Military notables, 1969–1971

Charles L. Singleton, US Army service dates: July 23, 1969—April 26, 1971

Locations of military service: Fort Gordon and Fort Benning, Georgia; Republic of Vietnam: Phuoc Vinh, Bien Hoa, Saigon, and Nha Trang. Special duties and responsibilities: combat patrolling, intelligence, tactical operations, and leadership.

Sgt. (E-5) Charles L. Singleton, US Army, Tour 365, Reconnaissance, First Cavalry Division, Airmobile, Second Battalion, 12th Cavalry, May 25, 1970–April 25, 1971, Republic of Vietnam. During my tour of duty in South Vietnam, I survived several firefights and three ambushes. I was proud to fight and serve with combat-ready servicemen.

I thank these incredibly brave and hard-fighting soldiers of the Second Battalion, Reconnaissance Platoon, 12th Light Infantry Brigade (Airmobile), who always courageously served alongside me during my tour of duty in Vietnam. These combat soldiers were Rios; Samuel "Sam" Houston; J. J. Jones; Eddie "Lefty Bulldog Rifleman" Foster, Jerry, Cuddles, Rigger, a demolition genius; brave soldiers 1 and 2 (RPG, rocket-propelled grenade, shell shocked), good friend Savath Som, a Cambodian scout. Charlie Brown (killed in action); and specialist intelligence writer and great leader Maj. Sistrunk, battalion-bigrade tactical operations center (TOC).

Now, I'm ready to talk. While we were on a reconnaissance patrol, a North Vietnamese radio code in English was sent to us and requested our location. One soldier in my unit said to our RTO (radiotelephone operator) and lieutenant, "Don't SHACKLE," referring to ten-letter code words to map coordinates. The North Vietnamese fired mortar rounds at us trying to get us to call in artillery support from a neighboring army firebase. While this was going on, I kept saying to myself, *I hope and pray I won't go home in a body bag.* That day, my fellow squad member's timely advisement helped to secure our location and saved our lives.

Read "A Vietnam Soldier's Story, Body Bags" by Dr. Charles L. Singleton, in *I'm Ready to Talk*, by Robert O. Babcock.

Military notables included: Pacesetters Award, 492 Points first place; physical combat proficiency test, Fort Gordon, Georgia, 1969; Vietnam Combat Infantry Badge, National Defense Service Medal, Vietnam Service Medal, Vietnam Air Medal, Vietnam Campaign Medal, Army Commendation Medal, Bronze Star, Purple Heart,

Distinguished Army Rifle Shooting Badge, and the State of Georgia Certificate of Honor Service Medal, Vietnam War. Honorably discharged, July 1, 1975. USA Vietnam War Commemoration 2020: Vietnam Veteran lapel pin.

I dedicate my Vietnam story to my late brother, Sgt. Clement Albert Singleton Jr. (1941–2019), who served with the Second Battalion of the 28th Infantry Regiment, First Infantry Division (Big Red One), Republic of Vietnam, Black Lions Battalion, 1965, brave brother, and my young cousin (KIA), Pfc. William Thomas Smith (1948–1969), A Battery, First Battalion, 30th Artillery, First Cavalry Division. Tommy was killed in Vietnam on August 12, 1969.

Vietnam. Photo credit: First Team Productions, W. T. Smith   Clement Albert Singleton Jr.   William Thomas Smith

The Healing Game: A Vietnam Soldier's Story. Since 1970, US Army First Cavalry Division, Airmobile, Sgt. Charles L. Singleton, Republic of Vietnam (RVN), 5-25-1970–4-25-1971

Atlanta History Center Veterans History Project, Oral History and Genealogy, Atlanta. Otis Redding, John Lee Hooker, and Van Morrison, "Don't Look Back, The Healing Game"

Veterans History Project Interview, Friday, January 17, 2020 by Sue VerHoef, director of Oral History and Genealogy, William Joseph Bruckner, and Cary S. King of the Atlanta Vietnam Veterans Business Association.

A Vietnam Soldier's Story, US Army, First Cavalry Division, Airmobile, Sgt. Charles L. Singleton, South Vietnam, 1970–1971, Tahesha Brown, literary DVD PowerPoint technical consultant, November 9, 2019

I'm Ready to Talk: Vietnam Veterans Preserve Their Stories. "Some 160-plus veterans' personal stories from members of the Atlanta Vietnam Veterans Business Association (AVVBA), who answered our nation's call to fight in Vietnam between 1959 and 1975. Stories come from all branches of our military and cover the war from the DMZ to the Delta, and those who served in the waters of the South China Sea and flew from bases in surrounding countries. "Vietnam Soldier's Story, Body Bags," by Dr. Charles L. Singleton, in "I'm Ready to Talk," Robert Babcock, November 26, 2019.

Spotlight on Local Author: A National Bestselling Book, Read Between the Lines, Provocative Essays for Saving Our children by Dr. Charles L. Singleton, September 27, 2019

The Healing Game: A Vietnam Soldier's Story, from 1970 to 2021, by Dr. Charles L. Singleton

Reference Tour 365 The Republic of Vietnam Service, Published by the US Army, summer 1970, APO San Francisco.

The Family Journal, USA & Overseas: Sarah McLean, editor; Karen Merrilles, communications editor; Isreal T. Singleton, editor in review; Charles L. Singleton, publisher, 2005–2021

Vietnam Veterans Oral History Project at Young Harris College. Interview by B. Lee, March, July 1, 2002, transcription draft, July 24, 2002. "And thus the soldier arm'd with resolution told his tale." —Colley Gibber

After a Viet Cong attack on a U.S. compound near Pleiku, American aircraft struck at NVA barracks just north of the 17th parallel, marking the first time the U.S. had bombed North Vietnam (below), Nguyen Van Thieu is sworn in as President of South Vietnam (right), and is honored at a parade celebrating the inauguration and National Day (left).

Sgt. Charles L. Singleton (on right), Tour 365 reconnaissance, at Base Camp 2, with best friend Staff Sgt. "Sam" Houston, Second Battalion, 12th Cavalry, May 25, 1970–April 25, 1971 in Vietnam.

"Tour 365—The Republic of Vietnam Service," published by the US Army, Summer 1970, APO San Francisco.

Sgt. Charles L. Singleton, Tour 365, page 22, May 25, 1970–April 25, 1971, "The Republic of Vietnam Under Attack," published by the US Army, summer 1970, APO San Francisco.

The Healing Game: A Vietnam Soldier's Story, since 1970, US Army, First Cavalry Division, Airmobile, Sgt. Charles L. Singleton, the Republic of Vietnam, 5-25-1970–4-25-1971: "Flashback Episodes before My Tour of Duty in the United States Army," The Singleton Family of Summerville, SC: military service, 1917 (105 years and counting).

1. Charles L. Singleton was a scholar athlete (football and track) and student council president at Elizabeth City State College (ECSC, later, Elizabeth City State University, ECSU). In the Central Intercollegiate Athletic Association (CIAA), Singleton was an All-CIAA halfback from 1966 to 1967. He was inducted into the ECSU Sports Hall of Fame (1999). Charles was also inducted into the Alston High School Athletic Hall of Fame (2000), in Summerville, South Carolina.

His early professional football affiliation (1968) was with the Westchester Bulls of the Atlantic Coast Football League (ACFL, the NFL's New York Giants' farm team), Mt. Vernon, New York, and the Brooklyn Golden Knights of the Semi-Professional League in Brooklyn.

Years later, Singleton completed successful professional football tryouts with the Birmingham Americans of the World Football League (WFL) at Morehouse College and Lakewood Stadium in Atlanta. However, Singleton decided to discontinue playing football after his military service and near-death Vietnam experience.

Muhammad Ali, the world's "greatest" conscientious objector's belief and image: Blogspot.com and Bing.com. "Ali's Vietnam decision was so influential."

The Healing Game: A Vietnam Soldier's Story, US Army First Cavalry Division, Airmobile, Sgt. Charles L. Singleton, South Vietnam, photo gallery, 1917 to 2019. Muhammad Ali 1967, 1968. Ali was the heavyweight boxing champion of the world. In 1967, he refused to be inducted into the military on religious grounds. Ali's Supreme Court case was *Clay v. United States*. In 1968–1969, I seriously thought about becoming a conscientious objector. (photo credit: Microsoft Bing, Muhammad Ali)

2. But I decided not to become a conscientious objector because of my family's history of dedicated military service (1917–1967). These members were from Metro Summerville, Ridgeville, and Charleston, South Carolina. My late oldest brother, Clement A. Singleton Jr. (1941–2019) and first cousin Tommy Smith (1948–1969, KIA Vietnam) served in Vietnam while I was a civilian.

The Singleton family members attended Alston High School (AHS). The AHS 1964 classmates and friends of the family, since World War I, from July 28, 1914 through November 11, 1918, are as follows. In World War I, there were granduncles Isom Singleton (1917–1918) and Lawrence Jones (died in 1917, World War I), and cousin James "Papa" W. Millhouse (1893–1962).

Likewise, James's son, Tillman U. Millhouse Sr. (1918–1986) served in World War II. These two were indeed very proud soldiers and veterans of Germantown, Summerville, South Carolina, since 1917. Tillman U. Millhouse Sr. was stationed at Pearl Harbor, Oahu, Hawaii, when Japan attacked the military port on December 7, 1941. Then there was a highly decorated cousin, Lawrence Jenkins (1917–2009), who served in World War II.

Next are the Singleton's in-laws of the Korean War from 1950 to 1953. They were three brothers, Amos Parker Myers (1927–2022), Edward Myers (1932–2013), and Marion Myers (1931–2009). They were also from Germantown, Summerville, South Carolina. Then there is Summerville, South Carolina's Rollins Edwards (1922–2017). In 1945, he was at Clark Air Base, Philippines. He was a World War II veteran (1939–1945) and survivor of the secret US Army World War II mustard gas experiments on African American soldiers.

A truly outstanding US civilian was Charles Singleton's father, Clement Addison Singleton Sr. (1913–2001). He was a part-time farmer and worked just short of thirty years for the federal government (1942–1972) in Charleston, South Carolina. He was in the Works Progress Administration, Ordinance Depot, Naval Shipyard, and Air Force Base. While he was employed at the Charleston Air Force Base, he was awarded the US Air Force Certificate of Safety for improving safety procedures in loading and unloading C-130 Hercules military transport aircraft.

In 2003, a portion of South Carolina Highway 61 in Dorchester County, from Walterboro Road to the southernmost intersection of Old Beech Hill Road, was named in his honor. Information can be found at www.scgeneralassembly. net/sess115_2003-2004/bills/469.htm.

Clement Singleton Senior and Junior were true students of learning and life. Please continue reading locally, nationally, and worldwide at http://www.blacknewsscoop.com/2020/02/c-l-singleton-writes-south-carolina.html.

Other relatives, in-laws, and friends who served were Mack Drayton Sr. (1911–1998), Isaac "Mossa" Drayton (1927–2005), and cousin Mack Drayton Jr. Then there was Eddie Lee Ganaway, Samuel Flood, Booker T. Flood, Clifford Flood, James L. Geddis, James McLean, Edward "Mullie" Samuels, and brothers Earvin Ryan Smith and Frederick L. Smith.

There were also 1964 AHS classmates who were Vietnam-era veterans: Lt. Col. Jordan Simmons; Airman Milton N. Hunt (1946–1999); Sgt. Roosevelt Gaymon Jr.; army specialist Sinclair Ladson (1946–1989); Staff Sgt. Charles D. Logan (1946–2021), 1st Sgt. Ezekiel Ancrum, air force; Henry Lee "Go Back Hollings" Hollands Sr.; and Ernest Samuel Moultrie, air force, Korean War veteran.

3. Military service members since the Vietnam War were/are Karen Merrilles, Ann Middleton King, Jerry Bell, Amos Myers, Harold Smith, Ronald Tucker, Cedric Tucker, Johnny Lee Mosley, Isaac Evans Jr., Jefferson "Bill" Evans, Jerry Quinn Greene Sr., Randy Caldwell, Jerrall Haynes, and Shawn Flood.

And presently in service are nephew Robert Perry Jr., Navy Master Chief E-9, USS *Hampton*, Othniel Evans, Senior Master Sergeant E-8, US Air Force, and Mellonie A. Jones, Technical Sergeant E-6, US Air Force (assistant manager, Joint Base, Charleston, DFAC). And there is Air Force Second Lieutenant Lauren Singleton, 2019, Clemson University, Columbia, South Carolina. In 2020, Lauren was studying medicine at Medical University South Carolina, Charleston, South Carolina.

Then there was the author of *Roots*, Alex Haley (1921–1992). In 1937, he attended State Normal School and was part of the fraternity brothers of the Lambda Gamma chapter of Omega Psi Phi fraternity, ECSU, Elizabeth City, North Carolina. Alex was in the US Coast Guard from 1939 to 1959.

Next was Lt. Col. Tyron Wallace Eason Sr., army instructor, ROTC, and Cpt. Anthony "Tony" Swain, US Navy. Anthony was part of the Brotherhood of Military Inductees of ECSU Lambda Gamma chapter. Then there is Robert L. "Bobby" Vaughan (1928–2021), Little Coach, US Army, Korean War; and Nathaniel Grant Jr., US Army. Nathaniel was my Omega Psi Phi brother and lifetime friend. From 1967 to 1968, he was ECSC student council campaign manager, student advisor, and my classmate.

At ECSU in 1968, my fellow army classmates were Samuel Jeter, co-captain of the Vikings Football Team and part of the US Army's 82nd Airborne Division, Vietnam. Next was Herman "Pompey" Horne Jr. (1947–2011) and my college roommate, Thomas Evans Jr. (1947–2021).

The ECSC Vikings football teammates who were US Army veterans were Col. Otha Sydnor, Sylvester "Vet" Clinton Bynum (1944–2020), Jethro C. Williams (1940–2018), Benny O'Donald Hodges (1942–2010; US Army Airborne Division and ECSC football/track coach), Willie "TX" Gafney, Eugene "Gene Gogo" Thompson, and Ronald Leigh.

4. Jordan M. Simmons III, of Summerville, South Carolina, attended ECSC in '68 and survived the Orangeburg massacre on February 8, 1968—turbulent times. Yes, looking back, we as a community in 1968 lived with social unrest. This was before and after the untimely assassination of Martin Luther King Jr., on April 4, 1968. On February 8, 1968, at ECSC, two hundred protesters were demonstrating against racial segregation at the local bowling alley.

Afterward, on campus, three African American male protesters were killed and twenty-eight other student protestors were wounded by South Carolina Highway Patrol officers. During this death-driven tragedy, my fellow 1964 AHS classmate and track teammate, Jordan M. Simmons III, was brought down with a single shot to his neck. It missed his aorta and spine.

Amazingly, after his miraculous, near-death experience at the Orangeburg massacre, Simmons III graduated from college and joined the US Army. He bravely served in Vietnam (1970–1971) with the 101st Airborne Division (Screaming Eagles) as an infantry platoon leader and company executive officer. He also courageously served in the Gulf War (Desert Storm) in 1991 as an intelligence information systems officer.

Lt. Col. Simmons, a twenty-nine-year army veteran, retired in 1998 (*Alston High School Garnet & Blue 1964 Journal Classic Stories*, 2014–2022).

You can revisit the "Orangeburg Massacre—Survivors Tell Their Stories" at https://www.youtube.com/watch?v=hWMqf68mLAc. And you can continue reading about ECSC civil rights challenges and achievements some fifty-four years ago by ECSC students in "A Time of Mourning," Elizabeth City, North Carolina, April 7, 1968: http://www.blacknewsscoop.com/2020/10/learn-why-hbcu-scholar-dr-charles-l.html.

On April 7, 1968, only three days after Martin Luther King Jr.'s assassination, a nonviolent and peaceful march was successfully organized at ECSC. It ended at the Pasquotank County Courthouse, Elizabeth City, North Carolina. Plus, there were my speeches: "Stay the Course" and "The Cross of Freedom."

Students attended their classes; they did not walk out of school in protest of the assassination of Martin L. King Jr. And yes, Charles L. Singleton's family members, relatives, and friends celebrated "Our Heritage and Military Service in the USA and Overseas since 1914." Absolutely 108 consistent years of our military dedication, sacrifice, and duty. (*The Family Journal, USA & Overseas*, since 2004)

The Healing Game: A Vietnam Soldier's Story, US Army First Cavalry Division, Airmobile, Sgt. Charles L. Singleton, Vietnam, May 25, 1970–April 25, 1971: "Flashback Episodes Before, During, and After My Tour of Duty in the US Army," *The Singleton Family of Summerville, South Carolina: Military Service, 1917 (105 Years and Counting)*.

5. I graduated from ECSC on May 26, 1968. My family and friends from South Carolina to New York City attended and celebrated a grand event in Elizabeth City, North Carolina. I was the first in my birth family to graduate from college. After graduating, I lived in Brooklyn with Ermine Singleton Myers, my sister (1936–2020), Marion Myers, her husband (1931–2009), and Bernard Myers, their young son.

Marion Myers lived in Germantown, Summerville, South Carolina, and was one of three Myers brothers in the Korean War. Amos, Edward, and brother-in-law Marion Myers were Germantown's Korean War Veterans of Summerville, South Carolina. With three sons in the army at the same time (Korean War 1950–1953), the Myers brothers' parents, James Myers Jr. and Elizabeth Herrington Myers, must have had many sleepless nights, and prayerful thoughts for their sons. After the three years of war, Amos, Edward, and Marion were honorably discharged with distinction.

These three extraordinary brothers, who attended AHS during the 1950s, were highly influential in my decisions to attend college, play football, and try out for the Westchester Bulls Atlantic Coast Football League and the NFL's New York Giants. Marion and Edward thought that by trying out with the Westchester Bulls, I would significantly increase my chances of playing with the New York Giants.

They reminded me often that Ronnie Blye, New York Giants halfback no. 45 (Notre Dame and Florida A&M), made his way after college into professional football by playing for the Westchester Bulls. Since I was not drafted by a professional football team after playing four years on the Vikings, the Elizabeth City State College football team, I walked on with the Westchester Bulls, who played their home games at Memorial Stadium in Mt. Vernon, New York.

I performed very well at the football camp for four weeks, but I did not survive the last cut. Twenty-two collegiate halfbacks tried out, and I was among the top five until the Giants management made a financial decision to let me go (no contract) because other players trying out had initially been drafted by the Giants. So the week before the season opener, Ed Kolman, the co-head coach of the Westchester Bulls, said to me, "Singleton, I'm not cutting you from the team. The New York Giants management is letting you go because they have to get their money's worth out of drafted players previously offered signing bonuses by the Giants during the 1968 NFL draft."

However, after my disheartening release from the Westchester Bulls, I had a standout, remarkable season of playing semipro ball with Al Glasco's Brooklyn Golden Knights (TCFL) in Brooklyn. I also taught English to teens with behavioral as well as reading problems in Bedford-Stuyvesant at Stephen Decatur Junior High, PS 35, 1968–1969). Open Highways English Book, "How the Impossible Becomes Possible in New York English Classroom."

After school, I worked at the Brownsville Community Center in Brooklyn with Harry Eli, the center's director. In summer 1969, I, SSN 3818475, was drafted into the US Army by the Dorchester County Draft Board after several letters were written about my teaching success with these special children by school administrators of PS 35.

6. After I was drafted, I returned home to spend precious time with my family: father, Clement Addison Singleton Sr. (1913–2001; mother, Catherine Elizabeth "Queen" Flood Singleton (1916–1990); brothers Clement A. Singleton Jr. (1941–2019), Benjamin J. Singleton Sr. (1943–2017), and Isreal T. Singleton; sisters Thelma Singleton Evans (1934–1982), Sarah Singleton McLean and niece, Marjorie Singleton Samuels (1951–2007); and Alston High School (AHS) 1964 classmates and friends.

I was disappointed that upon my returning home to Summerville, I did not get a chance to meet with my former AHS football coach, Jimmy Greene (1939–2009). He was a scholar athlete, sports star, and legendary scholastic, collegiate, and professional football player (Benedict College, Columbia, South Carolina, 1957–1962, and the Montreal Allouettes, Canadian Football League, 1962). While coaching football at AHS (1962–1965, 38–6 win record, 86 percent), he was an amazing educator and mentor.

On Wednesday, July 23, 1969, I arrived at the Trailways bus stop in Summerville, which was the OK grocery store. I purchased a one-way ticket to Columbia, South Carolina—Fort Jackson, US Army—for basic combat training. On my way, I prayed that I would return safely one day.

At Fort Jackson, I received the bald military haircut and army fatigues and was told that as an enlistee E-1, I would be making $109.50 a day, "once a month." *Oh, I finally made it*, I thought. I'd have a chance to be drafted by the Green Bay Packers out of the army! (Smile).

Sadly, with my new professional guaranteed contract, upon completing basic training, I along with many other draftees were bused to Fort Gordon near Augusta, Georgia. I successfully completed basic training thus reflecting my previous scholastic and collegiate accomplishments. I scored first on the physical combat proficiency test, successfully completed advanced infantry training at Fort Gordan, and was selected to attend the Noncommissioned Officer Academy (NCOA), a military school in Fort Benning. After completing NCO school, I was assigned to teach and tutor NCO attendees map reading skills and combat intelligence and military operations as directed by Sergeant First Class Morton, E-7, who served and survived two tours in Vietnam combat.

Pfc. Charles L. Singleton, US Army, 1969, basic training, Fort Gordon, Augusta, Georgia. Company E, 2BN, First TNG BDE. Most Outstanding Physical Fit of 500–800 soldiers. Photo credit: The Drug Years During Vietnam, YouTube.com.

Sgt. Charles L. Singleton, Fort Benning, Columbus, Georgia, 1970. *United States of America Soldier Ready! The Reality of Combat in Vietnam, My 16 Life and Death Episodes: 5-25-1970–4-25-1971* (Vietnam War episodes). Vietnam body bags: Bing.com

7. Bien Hoa Air Base, South Vietnam. I saw piles of garbage bags that turned out to be body bags. Vietnam, 1970. Bing "Like" Images.

8. Army sergeant. Tour 365, Republic of Vietnam Service, 2nd. 12th Airmobile Company Flag: Before going on my first patrol.

9. Army sergeant. Tour 365, Republic of Vietnam Service, Combat Landing LZ—Machete Knife Readiness, helicopter pad, RVN, 1970. Viet Cong, the AK-47.

10. "NCO Shake and Bake," Private Rios told me one day shortly after arriving at Fire Base Nancy, southeast of Quang Tri and northwest of Hue, South Vietnam. On our first ground patrols, he would repeatedly call me a Shake and Bake sergeant. Rios taught me so much about fighting in Vietnam. He would often remind me that some members in our combat intelligence and reconnaissance squad were not good at walking point or leading us on the ground. His favorite quote was, "Shake and Bake, I'm getting short; my time fighting in Vietnam is almost over!"

11. Montagnard, or GIs' Mountain Yard, indigenous people, central highlands of Vietnam. Intelligence saved our lives one day. They said one night, near their mountain village, "Beaucoup Viet Cong and NVA [North Vietnamese Army soldiers] were traveling nearby, "No same, same me; no same, same you!" We took their advice, and were quickly evacuated back to a much safer area. Later, the air force via the army used our report concerning the Montagnards' observations to successfully bomb the suspected area that a battalion of NVA was occupying.

12. Do Not Walk on Trails or Cross Open Fields without Cover Fire. Well, one September day in 1970, my combat intelligence infantry squad, six to eight soldiers, walked out of the camouflaged jungle's dense foliage into an open field and were fired on by Viet Cong with AK-47s. We grounded ourselves; bullets continued to land all around us. During this sudden exchange of gunfire with our M16 rifles and M60 machine gun, Private Eddie "Bulldog" Foster (Florida) avoided getting struck by enemy bullets while rolling on the ground from side to side and shooting his weapon lying on his back.

Shortly after this encounter, the Viet Cong attackers moved away from the area. From that day forward, we called Eddie Foster Chuck Connors, the Rifleman. All throughout this ambush, I too rolled on the ground, and ducked bullets to avoid being placed in a body bag and ending up at Bien Hoa Air Base.

13. After this near-death experience, I realized that had I died, the news would have killed my mother, Catherine, and father, Clement Sr. In the late 1940s, my mother was carrying me and suffering with asthma. At the Old Dorchester

County Hospital (1937–1980s) in Summerville, the doctor attending my mother told my father that he could not see how my mother was going to give birth to me with her failing lung condition. My father said, "If that's the case, let them die in our two-room house on Red Road."

In 1970, if I had died in Vietnam, my father, a C-130 Hercules civilian loadmaster employee at Charleston Air Force Base, would have been so disappointed that his Charles was killed and then placed in a body bag on a C-130 Hercules. It would have been too much for my father to handle. Read more here: "A Vietnam Soldier's Story, Body Bags," by Dr. Charles L. Singleton, page 444 in "I'm Ready to Talk (Vietnam)," Tour 365, 1970–1971, Republic of Vietnam, during combat, Robert O. Babcock.

14. Outdoor pit latrine, toilet ditch, Firebase Nancy, US Army and Army of the Republic of Vietnam (ARVN) Base, Southeast of Quang Tri, Vietnam. Seemingly days after the September 1970 open-field crossing and subsequent firefight, we were waiting for our next recon (reconnaissance) assignment when the North Vietnam Army (NVA) and Viet Cong launched a surprise mortar attack. During it, I seriously thought about taking cover in the pit latrine. As the attack subsided, I decided that I did not have to jump into it.

15. October 7, 1970: *Red Badge of Courage* (Stephen Crane, 1871–1900) and my Purple Heart day. Crane's Henry Fleming, who earlier had run from a battle in shame, regretted his cowardice and wanted desperately to be wounded so he could receive a red badge of courage. Unlike Henry Fleming, I did not want to be wounded. However, on Wednesday, October 7, 1970, after receiving a shrapnel injury (burns and bruises) and concussion from a "chicom" grenade explosion, Rigger, a demolition genius, and I were injured along with others as we were protecting our bomb-crater position.

The more seriously injured of our platoon were medevacked by Huey helicopters. My platoon (two squads, fifteen soldiers) was pinned down for hours by Viet Cong snipers. During the firefight, we were initially supported by AH-1 Cobra gunships. However, the gunships were ineffective because the enemy, after shooting at us from surrounding trees and tall vegetation, would return to their underground bunkers. A second lieutenant who was a forward observer from South Carolina State College in Orangeburg was called into battle. He coordinated a barrage of army cannon at Firebase Nancy and navy artillery long-range guns off the central coast of Vietnam.

Hallelujah! It worked! As the night came upon us, the firefight ceased; that was when the big-headed ants took over in our perimeter: *Pheidole megacephala* (*fabricius*). After being repeatedly bitten and stung by these ants, a number of us shouted expletive after expletive, profanities, and four-letter words. Those ants kept us awake, and NVA and Viet Cong sappers were not able to attack us while we were resting and sleeping.

16. Napalm—liquid fire. After almost losing my life in October 7 1970, we were on patrol in early November 1970 when a call came in on the RTO (radiotelephone) that napalm bombs were going to be dropped possibly miles away from our position. We were silent and stealthy. Then all of a sudden, the napalm bombs exploded and sucked the oxygen out of the air surrounding us! Quora and Tour 365 photo images, Republic of Vietnam, 1970–1971.

Napalm bombs, Vietnam 1968. istockphoto.com.

Photo credit: US Soldiers and RVN 1970: Viet Cong, the AK-47, public domain

PHOTO BY SPEC. 5 GORDON GAHAN

PHOTO BY SPEC. 4 JOHN HOSIER

A sniper firing on U.S. soldiers draws a return blast (above). Soldiers protect their ears from the blast of a mortar round leaving its tube (right).

Sgt. Charles L. Singleton, Tour 365, page 28, May 25, 1970–April 25, 1971, Republic of Vietnam, combat action. Photos by Spec. 5. Gordon Gahan and Spec. 4 John Hosier, brave combat photographers.

Photo credit: Spec. 5 Gordan Gahan, Tour 365, Republic of Vietnam Service, published by the US Army, summer 1970, APO San Francisco.

Sgt. Charles L. Singleton. Tour 365, Republic of Vietnam Service, 2nd. 12th Airmobile.

17. First nighttime ambush reconnaissance. In late November, our recon platoon went on a nighttime patrol. When it was time for my squad (five or six of us) to go on duty, my best friend, Staff Sgt. Samuel "Sam" Houston, volunteered to go with us though he was not assigned to do so. Throughout the night, Sam made sure that we stayed alert. He kept reminding us that this was his third tour in Vietnam: combat intelligence, learning is staying alive, quiet stealth, camouflage, no cigarette smoking on the perimeter while on duty at night. As a result of his timely knowledge about fighting at night in Vietnam, we got to see another day!

18. Early December 1970, RPG (rocket-propelled grenade) ambush. This Soviet weapon fired at us during a reconnaissance by a North Vietnamese Army or Viet Cong soldier came awfully close to killing us. It barely missed the head of a sergeant who was walking point. Quickly, we pulled the sergeant to the ground and gave him cover fire in the direction the RPG had come from. Following that brief but life-threatening encounter, we had to medivac the sergeant, who became a mental casualty because of this near-death experience.

19. Christmas Eve, December 1970, Black Virgin Mountain cease-fire surprise. The week before the Thursday, December 24, 1970, Vietnam cease-fire, Tây Ninh Province, Vietnam, Nui Ba Den (Black Virgin Mountain), our platoon, Second Battalion, 12th Cavalry Air Mobility was on standby to support US combat troops fighting in the

area. Charlie Alpha: While we waited our turn to be helicoptered or transported into combat that fatal day up the Black Virgin Mountain, much to our surprise, the heliborne assault was called off because of the number of friendly casualties.

20. January 1971, Cambodia, Missing in Action, Presumption of Death finding. In early January 1971, my platoon was given new maps coordinates and helicoptered into Cambodia. Our combat assignment consisted of gathering information and looking for a US Air Force Phantom fighter jet that had been shot down by a North Vietnam surface-to-air missile. After searching in thick vegetation in the mountains and mosquito-infested jungles for several days and nights, we were unsuccessful in locating the jet and pilots.

21. January 1971, R&R, Taipei, Taiwan. During my eighth month in South Vietnam, I selected Taipei for my well-deserved rest, recovery, relaxation, recreation, and rehabilitation. Upon arriving in Taipei, I quickly learned that converting US dollars into Taiwanese dollars was an outstanding currency swap. I was able to eat in upscale Chinese restaurants, buy tailored suits—"You draw, I make," said the Taiwanese tailor.
R&R highlights were as follows.

- Do not mention Chairman Mao Zedong's *Little Red Book.*
- The catch of the day at restaurants included everything caught by Chinese fishermen that day—all types of seaweed and octopuses, snakes, and crabs.
- Gigantic movie theaters sold fried chicken feet instead of popcorn.
- Teenagers repeatedly defeated American R&R vacationers in table tennis for $1. Rich kids!
- Chinese entertainers' perfectly imitated sounds included "The Night Train" (James Brown), "Yesterday" (the Beatles), and "Sittin' on the Dock of the Bay" (Otis Redding).

22. January 1971–April 1971, Army tactical operation center brigade and battalion assignment and early out. After I returned from R&R, I was assigned to army intelligence and operations until my early out, the end of my military duty in Vietnam ordered by President Nixon. Specialist intelligence writer and great TOC leader Maj. Sistrunk, Battalion-Brigade Tactical Operations Center, thank you! My active combat tour in South Vietnam ended on April 25, 1971.

I returned home after being discharged in Oakland, California, and I was looked down upon by some passengers on a civilian flight from San Francisco to Charleston Airport. (*The Healing Game*, "1971 to Present").

Dr. Charles L. Singleton, Atlanta VA Health Care System (AVAHCS), Research Volunteer of the Year, 2019–2020.

The Atlanta VA Center for Visual and Neurocognitive Rehabilitation (CVNR) Research Team with Dr. Joe Nocera, Department of Neurology, School of Medicine, Emory University; Dr. Charles L. Singleton, Clinical and Educational

Research Consultant; Holly Hudson, Research Study Coordinator, Certified Clinical Research Coordinator (CCRC); Kevin Mammino, Health Science Specialist (CCRC). Singleton's clinical research was inspired by Dr. Keith McGregor.

AVAHCS press release,

Singleton is a CVNR Atlanta VA Health Care System Community Advisory panelist (April 16, 2021).

Highly Decorated Veteran And HBCU Wellness Educator Charles Singleton Awarded Atlanta VA Health Care System Research Volunteer of the Year: Trending Nationwide & Overseas: C. L. Singleton, Atlanta VA Health Care System Facebook Posting: https://www.facebook.com/AtlantaVAHCS/

On May 14, 2019, The Atlanta VA Health Care System Recognized The Outstanding Research Volunteer of The Year Recipient (Atlanta VA Research Day, May 14, 2019, at the U. S. Department of Veterans Affairs), Atlanta VA Medical Center, 1670 Clairmont Road, Decatur, Georgia 30033. The first annual Atlanta VA Health Care System Research Volunteer Of The Year Award was presented to Dr. Charles Singleton last week by Atlanta VAHCS Interim Director Dr. Ajay Dhawan. Dr. Singleton, a Vietnam Veteran and Purple Heart recipient, was nominated by the research team at the Atlanta VAHCS Visual and Neurocognitive Rehabilitation (CVNR).

He is a passionate volunteer who participated in an extensive research study over the course of six months and motivated his fellow research participants with his enthusiasm and dedication for the program in the process. In addition to participating in the study, Dr. Singleton volunteers with research related activities including writing an article about his experience as a research participant for the Center newsletter and making a detailed journal about his experience to share with other Veterans and research participants.

Speaking at the event, Associate Chief of Staff for Research, Dr. C. Michael Hart, acknowledges that research participants "selflessly and altruistically give their time, energy, (and sometimes samples) to enable the process of biomedical research. Without volunteers for clinical research studies, the pace of progress and understanding in treating human disease would be significantly impaired. We are all thankful for and indebted to these volunteers."

Dr. Singleton is a 1968 graduate of Elizabeth City State College (ECSC), now Elizabeth City State University (ECSU), a 1972 graduate of Atlanta University (AU): Clark Atlanta University (CAU), and a Nova Southeastern University 1993 Doctoral alumnus. Respectfully, Singleton is a Vietnam Era Veteran (Purple Heart), who authored a chapter of the Vietnam Veterans' Oral History Project at Young Harris College, 2002, and the Veterans History Project at Kenan Re-search Center, Atlanta History Center, Friday, January 17, 2020. He is a member Georgia Writers Association (GWA) and the Atlanta Vietnam Veterans Business Association (AVVBA). Dr. Singleton, educator, author, journalist, researcher, and wellness consultant, for the past 29 years of his 55 years of writing, teaching and publishing, has been an extraordinary community volunteer in clinical and historical research (65 Studies). Read the Atlanta VA Center for Visual & Neurocognitive Rehabilitation (CVNR) Newsletter, New Project Focus: Protection of the Brain by Chemical Hypothermia, Shan Ping Yu, MD, PhD, and Participant Perspective: Effects of Exercise Intervention on Aging Related Motor Decline by Charles Singleton, D.Ed. PDF Page 3. www.varrd.emory.edu/media/cms_page_media/207/CVNR_Newsletter_Winter%202015_FinalEdition_FEB2015.pdf or visit Your Fantastic Mind at the Atlanta VA Center for Visual & Neurocognitive Rehabilitation (CVNR).

"A Vietnam War Purple Heart Awardee and Bestselling Author Writes about Saving Our Children" https://www.blacknewsscoop.com/2020/01/a-vietnam-soldier-and-bestselling.html.

"We Honor Your Speech History, Speak More" by HBCU author, clinical researcher, and Educator Dr. Charles L. Singleton. http://www.blacknewsscoop.com/2021/01/learn-how-to-honor-your-speech-history.html.

Vietnam books, *I'm Ready to Talk* and *I'm Ready to Talk Two*: *Vietnam Vets Preserve Their Stories*, Robert O. "Bob" Babcock. https://www.deedspublishing.com/store. It is our earthly hope as godly human beings that we live healthy lives in everlasting peace, joy, and posterity.

The Healing Game: A Vietnam Soldier's Story, US Army First Cavalry Division, Airmobile, Sgt. Charles L. Singleton, Republic of South Vietnam, 5-25-1970—4-25-1971.

Looking back at the turbulent days and times of uncertainty during the 1960s, I was drafted into military service after receiving four deferments while I was in college. I served in the army so American citizens could enjoy the freedoms and liberties of living in a country where one could stand up, sit down, kneel, or pray during ceremonies when and where our national anthem was being played as long as one's action did not interfere with the inalienable rights of others.

As Americans, we have the right to appeal, disagree, dissent, and protest.
In Vietnam, I fought for the people of the brave and proud United States of America.
The preamble to the United States Constitution, written over 234 years ago, reads,
We the People of the United States, in Order to form a more perfect Union, establish Justice, insure domestic Tranquility, provide for the common defense, promote the general Welfare, and secure the Blessings of Liberty to ourselves and our Posterity, do ordain and establish this Constitution for the United States of America."

Charles L. Singleton and Samuel Houston on patrol, Vietnam

Charles L. Singleton and Savath Som, base camp, RVN

The Healing Game: A Vietnam Soldier's Story, "*The Healing Game,*" US Army, First Cavalry Division, Airmobile, Sgt. Charles L. Singleton, Vietnam, 5-25-1970–4-25-1971.

Here I am again, back on the corner again.
Back where I belong. Where I've always been.
Everything the same. It don't ever change.
I'm back on the corner again. In the healing game.

—Van Morrison and John Lee Hooker, "The Healing Game." Photo credit: discog.com

Don't look back to the days of yesteryear. You cannot live on in the past.
Don't look back. And live on in the future.
—Photo and lyrics, Bing.com, "Singleton's PTSD-Related Insomnia, PTSD, RVN 1970."

Post-traumatic stress disorder

Newspaper photo caption submitted by Sally Jacobs Harmon, '73, Elizabeth City State University, June 6, 2019. REM sleep: in Dr. Charles L. Singleton's "PTSD-Related Insomnia: Post Traumatic Stress Disorder, Shirley LaForce, Readjustment Counselor."

"Yes, Sometimes I Can't Sleep, So I Write." ITs at the Atlanta Vet Center, College Park, Georgia, March 4, 2016 to present, counseling Superman Dr. Charles L. Singleton's "Sleepless" PTSD. — Photos, Standard Public Use

Tour 365, The Republic of Vietnam Service, US Army, summer 1970, APO San Francisco.

Sgt. Charles L. Singleton, Tour 365, page 22, May 25, 1970–April 25, 1971, "The Republic of Vietnam Under Attack," US Army, summer 1970, APO San Francisco

Superman's Psychiatrist Treating Him for Post-Traumatic Stress Disorder (PTSD) after Superman helped and saved so many others. Cartoon Parade Parade.com cartoons, December 28, 2008, artist Dan Piraro.

The Healing Game: A Vietnam Soldier's Story, "Remember Me, PTSD-Related Insomnia."

Whoa, you know I'm like a ship that's tossed and driven, oh, Lord, battered by an angry sea. Whoa, Lord, you know when the storms of life keep on ragin, 'Father, remember me. Oh, Lord, and sometimes it feels like the weight of the world is on my shoulders, whoa, yes it does; sometimes

Vietnam Veterans Memorial, Three Soldiers, bronze statue, Washington, DC, by Frederick Hart, Veterans Day, November 11, 1984

I'm burdened down in sorrow and misery, whoa, Lord, you know when the storms of life keep on ragin,' and I know it will, please remember me.

Oh, Lord, they tell me you, I know you. You remembered old Daniel, oh, yes you did. He was down in the lion's den. You made the lions back up, and let old Daniel go free. Oh, yes you did. You know when the storms of life keep on ragin,' do me like you did Daniel, remember me.

Whoa, Lord, I read about it. I read about how you remembered the Hebrews, oh, yes you did. They were down in the fiery furnace. It was seven times hotter than it ought to be, whoa, yes it was. You know when the storms of life keep on ragin,' do me like you did the Hebrews, and remember me.

Oh, Lord, remember me. Remember me father when I'm worried. Remember me father when you see me burdened down and lonely. Whoa, Lord, let me tell you father, when the storms of life keep on ragin,' Jesus, Father if you love me, remember me.

"Lord, Remember Me," Sam Cooke and the Soul Stirrers, Ace (1964), Musixmatch Songwriters Abkco Music.

Clement Albert Singleton Jr. (1941–2019), my dearly beloved brother, served during the Vietnam War as a sergeant in the US Army's First Infantry Division (Big Red 1), Black Lions Battalion (1965). Clement was a brave soldier, best friend, and war hero.

Jordan Simmons Army Lieutenant Colonel   Milton N. Hunt U.S. Airforce Airman 1946-1999 JBSC   Roosevelt Gaymon, Jr. U. S. Army Sergeant Sugar Hill, SC AHS

Jordan Simmons Orangeburg Massacre, 68   Sinclair Ladson U.S. Army Specialist, Vietnam AHS   Roosevelt Gaymon, Jr. U. S. Army Sergeant: Japan SH AHS

SSG Charles D. Logan U.S. Army   1SG Ezekiel Ancrum U.S . Army, 37 Years   SGT Charles L. Singleton U.S. Army AHS RVN

Henry Lee Hollings, Alston High School, 1964. Henry Hollands Sr., 2022, US military service veteran, AHS, Summerville, SC. US Air Force, January 6, 1946–May 16, 2022, distinguished Vietnam-era veteran

Basketball legend "Go Back" Henry Lee Hollings, Alston High School, 1964, Summerville, South Carolina, So Proud, '64

Mack Drayton Sr. (1911–1998) and wife, Emma Smalls Drayton (US Army, World War II veteran), Mack Jr., and Brother Isaac (1927–2005)

Korean War soldiers: brothers Amos Parker Myers (1927–2022), Edward Myers (1932–2013), and Marion Myers (1931–2009), US Army, 1950–1953

Cousin James "Papa" W. Millhouse (1893–1962), who served in World War I, and his son, Tillman U. Millhouse Sr. (1918–1986), World War II, were two proud soldiers and veterans of Summerville, South Carolina, since 1914.

Tillman U. Millhouse Sr. was stationed at Pearl Harbor, Oahu, Hawaii, when Japan attacked it on December 7, 1941.

Isom Singleton, World War I soldier, July 28, 1914–November 11, 1918, grand uncle of Vietnam veteran Sgt. Charles L. Singleton. Family photos, *The Family Journal, USA and overseas.*

Printed in the United States
by Baker & Taylor Publisher Services